EASY

Design by Ferosa Harold

Size

About 52 x 63 inches

Materials

Fine (sport) weight yarn,
   35 oz (2975 yds, 1050g) white
Note: *Our photographed afghan was made with Red Heart Soft Baby, White #700.*
Size B/1/2.25mm crochet hook or
   size required for gauge
Tapestry needle

Gauge

6 blocks x 7 rows = 3 inches

Pattern Stitches

Beginning mesh (beg mesh)

Ch 5 *(counts as a dc and a ch-2 sp)*, sk next 2 chs, dc in next dc.

Mesh

Ch 2, sk next 2 chs or dc, dc in next dc.

Block

Dc in next 2 chs or dc, dc in next dc, or, dc in next 3 dc.

Lacet

Dc in next dc, ch 3, sk next 2 dc, sc in next dc, ch 3, sk next 2 dc, dc in next dc.

Long Block

Dc in next dc, ch 5, sk next ch-3 sp, next sc and next ch-3 sp, dc in next dc.
Work odd-number rows on chart from right to left; work even-number rows from left to right.

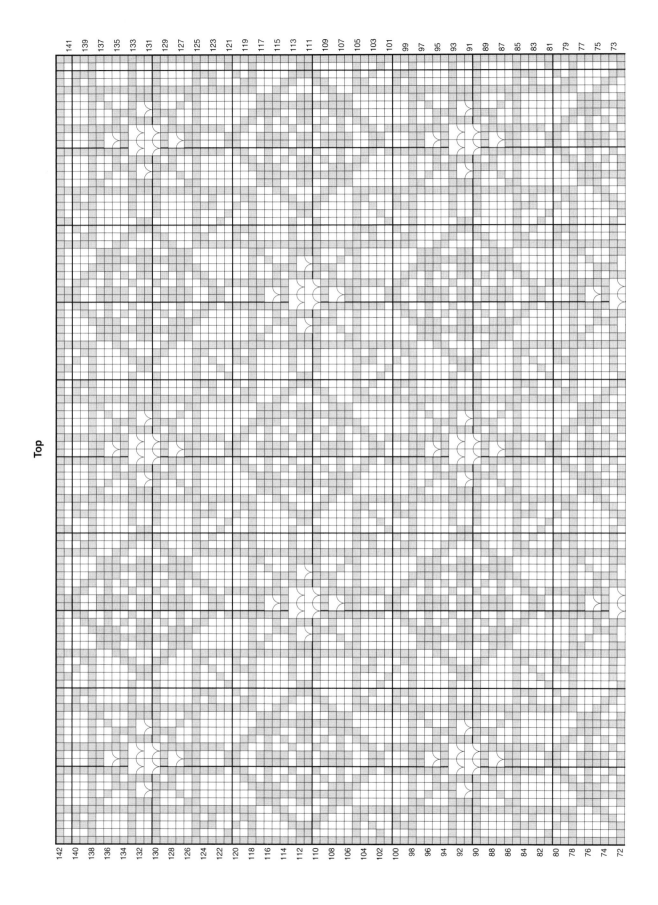

STITCH KEY
☐ Beg mesh or mesh
▨ Block
⧖ Lacet
☐ Long block

Bottom

Instructions

Ch 310.

Row 1 (WS): Dc in 5th ch from hook *(beg 4 skipped chs counts as a dc)* and in each rem ch. Turn.

Row 2 (RS): Ch 3 *(counts as a dc)*; * † dc in next 3 dc, [ch 2, sk next 2 dc, dc in next dc] 3 times; dc in next 3 dc, [ch 2, sk next 2 dc, dc in next dc] 4 times; dc in next 3 dc, [ch 2, sk next 2 dc, dc in next dc] twice; dc in next 3 dc, [ch 2, sk next 2 dc, dc in next dc] 4 times; dc in next 3 dc, [ch 2, sk next 2 dc, dc in next dc] 3 times †; dc in next 3 dc, [ch 2, sk next 2 dc, dc in next dc] twice; dc in next 3 dc, [ch 2, sk next 2 dc, dc in next dc] 5 times; dc in next 6 dc, [ch 2, sk next 2 dc, dc in next dc] 5 times; dc in next 3 dc, [ch 2, sk next 2 dc, dc in next dc] twice; rep from * once more, then rep from † to † once; dc in next 2 dc and in 4th ch of beg 4 skipped chs.

Rows 3–142: Follow charts on pages 2 and 3. At end of Row 142, do not fasten off.

EDGING

Rnd 1 (RS): Ch 8 *(counts as a dc and a ch-5 sp)*, dc in last dc made; working along next side, ch 5, sk next Row 142, dc in base of Row 141; † ch 5, sk next row, dc in base of next row †; rep from † to † to Row 2; ch 5, sk Row 2 and Row 1; working across next side in unused lps of beg ch, in first lp work (dc, ch 5, dc); †† ch 5, sk next 5 lps, dc in next lp ††; rep from †† to †† to last 6 unused lps; ch 5, sk next 5 lps, in next lp work (dc, ch 5, dc); working across next side, ch 5, sk Row 1, dc in top of next row; ††† ch 5, sk next row, dc in top of next row †††; rep from ††† to ††† to Row 141; ch 5, sk Row 141, in 3rd ch of beg ch-3 of Row 142 work (dc, ch 5, dc); working across row, †††† ch 5, sk next 5 dc, dc in next dc ††††; rep from †††† to †††† to last 6 dc; ch 2, sk next 5 dc; join with a dc in 3rd ch of beg ch-8.

Rnd 2: Ch 1, sc in sp formed by joining dc; * ch 8, sc in next ch-5 sp; rep from * around; ch 3; join with a dtr in first sc.

Rnd 3: Ch 1, in top of joining dtr work (sc, ch 3, sc); ch 3, in next ch-8 sp work (2 dc, ch 3, sl st in first ch, ch 1, 2 dc)—shell made; ch 3, shell in next ch-8 sp; † [ch 3, in next ch-8 sp work (sc, ch 3, sc); ch 3, shell in next ch-8 sp] 17 times; ch 3, in next ch-8 sp work (sc, ch 3, sc); [ch 3, in next ch-8 sp work (sc, ch 3, sc); ch 3, shell in next ch-8 sp] 18 times, ch 3, shell in next ch-8 sp; [ch 3, in next ch-8 sp work (sc, ch 3, sc); ch 3, shell in next ch-8 sp] 12 times; ch 3, in next ch-8 sp work (sc, ch 3, sc) †; [ch 3, in next ch-8 sp work (sc, ch 3, sc); ch 3, shell in next ch-8 sp] 13 times; ch 3, shell in next ch-8 sp; rep from † to † once; [ch 3, in next ch-8 sp work (sc, ch 3, sc); ch 3, shell in next ch-8 sp] 12 times; ch 3; join in first sc.

Fasten off and weave in ends.

Gentle Flowers

EASY

Design by Donna Collinsworth

Size
About 62 x 72 inches

Materials
Fine (sport) weight yarn,
   30 oz (2700 yds, 900g) white
Note: *Our photographed afghan was made with Bernat Softee Baby, White #2000.*
Size G/6/4mm crochet hook or size
   required for gauge
Size F/5/3.75mm crochet hook
Tapestry needle

Gauge
Small flower block = 3½ inches
   square

Pattern Stitches

Beginning cluster (beg cl)
Keeping last lp of each tr on hook, tr in 4 tr indicated, yo and draw through all 5 lps on hook.

Cluster (cl)
Keeping last lp of each tr on hook, tr in 5 tr indicated, yo and draw through all 6 lps on hook.

Instructions

Small Flower Block
(make 122)

Ch 4, join to form a ring.

Rnd 1: Ch 1, 12 sc in ring; join in first sc. (12 sc)

Rnd 2: Ch 4 *(counts as a tr on this and following rnds),* 4 tr in same sc; [ch 4, sk next 2 sc, 5 tr next sc] 3 times; ch 4, sk next 2 sc; join in 4th ch of beg ch-4.

Rnd 3: Ch 4, **beg cl** *(see Pattern Stitches)* over next 4 tr; ***** ch 5, in next ch-5 sp work (dc, ch 5, dc)—corner made; ch 5, **cl** *(see Pattern Stitches)* over next 5 tr; rep from ***** twice more; ch 5, in next ch-5 sp work (dc, ch 5, dc)—corner made; ch 5; join in 4th ch of beg ch-4.

Finish off and weave in ends.

Ribbed Block (make 48)

Ch 36.

Row 1: Dc in 3rd ch from hook *(beg 3 skipped chs count as a dc)* and in each rem ch. Turn. (34 dc)

Row 2: Ch 3 *(counts as a dc on this and following rows)*, working in back lps only, dc in each dc and in 3rd ch of beg 3 skipped chs. Turn.

Row 3: Ch 3, working in front lps only, dc in each dc and in 3rd ch of beg ch-3. Turn.

Rows 4–7: Rep Rows 2 and 3 twice more. At end of Row 7, do not turn.

Finish off and weave in ends.

Large Block (make 48)

With tapestry needle, sew one Small Flower Block to right side edge of each Ribbed Block.

Center Section

Note: *When sewing Large Blocks together, it is necessary to flip some to get correct placement of Small Flower Blocks.*

Referring to Diagram 1 for placement of blocks, sew 24 Large Blocks tog to form center section.

Edging

Hold center section with RS facing you; with smaller hook, make slip knot on hook and join with an sc in first st in upper right-hand corner.

Rnd 1: Ch 4, sc in same st—beg corner made; † [ch 4, sk next 2 sts, sc in next st] 11 times; [ch 4, sc in next ch-5 sp] 4 times; [ch 4, sk next 2 sts, sc in next st] 11 times; ch 4, sk next st, sc in next st, [ch 4, sc in next ch-5 sp] 3 times; ch 4, in next corner ch-5 sp work (sc, ch 4, sc)—corner made; working across next side, [ch 4, sc in next ch-5 sp] 3 times; [(ch 4, sc in end of next row) 7 times; (ch 4, sc in next ch-5 sp) 4 times] twice; [ch 4, sc in end of next row] 6 times; working across next side, ch 4 †; in first st work (sc, ch 4, sc)—corner made; rep from † to † once; ch 4; join in joining sc.

Rnd 2: Sl st in next ch-4 sp; in same sp work corner; * ch 4, † sc in next ch-4 sp, ch 4 †; rep from † to † to next corner; in corner ch-4 sp work corner; rep from * twice more; ch 4; rep from † to † to next corner; join in first sc.

Rnds 3–7: Rep Rnd 2.

Fasten off and weave in ends.

Inner Border Section

Referring to Diagram 2, sew rem Large Blocks tog.

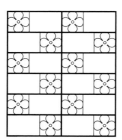

Diagram 1

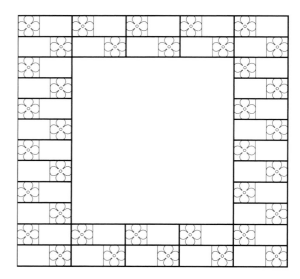

Diagram 2

Center and Border Assembly

Place center section inside inner border section. With tapestry needle, sew sections tog, easing to fit.

Border Edging

Hold piece with RS facing you; with smaller hook, make slip knot on hook and join with an sc in first st in upper right-hand corner.

Rnd 1: Ch 4, sc in same st—beg corner made; † [ch 4, sk next 2 sts, sc in next st] 11 times; [ch 4, sc in next ch-5 sp] 4 times; [ch 4, sk next 2 sts, sc in next st] 11 times; ch 4, sk next st, sc in next st, [ch 4, sc in next ch-5 sp] 3 times; ch 4, in next corner ch-5 sp work (sc, ch 4, sc)—corner made; working across next side, [ch 4, sc in next ch-5 sp] 3 times; [(ch 4, sc in end of next row) 7 times; (ch 4, sc in next ch-5 sp) 4 times] twice; [ch 4, sc in end of next row] 6 times; working across next side, ch 4 † ; in first st work (sc, ch 4, sc)—corner made; rep from † to † once; ch 4; join in joining sc.

Rnd 2: Sl st in next ch-4 sp; in same sp work corner; * ch 4, † sc in next ch-4 sp, ch 4 †; rep from † to † to next corner; in corner ch-4 sp work corner; rep from * twice more; ch 4; rep from † to † to next corner; join in first sc.

Rnds 3–5: Rep Rnd 2.

Fasten off and weave in ends.

Outer Border

Sew rem Small Flower Blocks tog in 2 rows of 21 blocks each and 2 rows of 16 blocks each. Sew rows tog to form outer border section.

Center Section and Outer Border Assembly

Place piece inside outer border section. With tapestry needle, sew sections tog, being careful not to twist flower blocks.

Border

Hold afghan with RS facing you and one long edge at top; with larger hook, join in upper right-hand corner ch-5 sp; ch 1, in same sp work (2 sc, ch 2, 2 sc)—corner made; † sc in next dc, 5 sc in next ch-5 sp, sc in next cl, 5 sc in next ch-5 sp; sc in next dc, 2 sc in next corner sp; sc in joining, 2 sc in next corner sp †; rep from † to † 19 times more; sc in next dc, 5 sc in next ch-5 sp, sc in next cl, 5 sc in next ch-5 sp; sc in next dc, in next corner ch-5 sp work (2 sc, ch 2, 2 sc)—corner made; rep from † to † 17 times; sc in next dc, 5 sc in next ch-5 sp, sc in next cl, 5 sc in next ch-5 sp; sc in next dc, in next corner ch-5 sp work (2 sc, ch 2, 2 sc)—corner made; rep from † to † 20 times; sc in next dc, 5 sc in next ch-5 sp, sc in next cl, 5 sc in next ch-5 sp; sc in next dc, in next corner ch-5 sp work (2 sc, ch 2, 2 sc)—corner made; rep from † to † 17 times; sc in next dc, 5 sc in next ch-5 sp, sc in next cl, 5 sc in next ch-5 sp; sc in next dc; join in first sc.

Fasten off and weave in ends.

Summer Lace

EASY

Design by Joyce Nordstrom

Size
About 52 x 63 inches

Materials
Medium (worsted) weight yarn, 44 oz (2200 yds, 1320g) off-white
Note: *Our photographed afghan was made with Red Heart TLC Amore, Vanilla #3103.*
Size I/9/5.5mm crochet hook or size required for gauge
Size J/10/6mm crochet hook

Gauge
9 X-sts = 8 inches

Pattern Stitches

Cross-Stitch (X-st)
Sk 2 sts indicated, dc in next st, ch 1, dc in first skipped st.

Cluster (cl)
In st indicated work (sc, hdc, dc).

Popcorn (pc)
5 dc in st indicated, drop lp from hook, insert hook in first dc, draw dropped lp through, ch 1.

Pattern Note
As the X-st rows may be tighter than the other rows, it may be easier to do these rows with the larger hook to keep the edges even. (Change to smaller hook on other rows.)

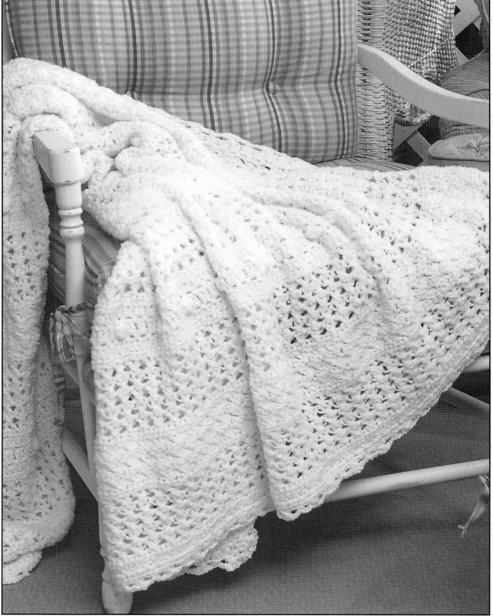

Instructions

With smaller hook, ch 172.

Foundation Row: Hdc in 3rd ch from hook and in each rem ch. Turn. *(170 hdc)*

Row 1 (RS): Ch 3, dc in first hdc; ***X-st** (*see Pattern Stitches*) over next 3 hdc; rep from ***** to last hdc; dc in last hdc. Turn. *(56 X-sts)*

Row 2: Ch 3, dc in first dc, X-st over each X-st; dc in last dc. Turn.

Rows 3–5: Rep Row 2.

Row 6: Ch 3, hdc in first dc, in each rem dc and in each ch-1 sp. Turn. *(170 hdc)*

Row 7: Ch 3, sc in first hdc; ***cl** (*see Patten Stitches*) in next hdc, sk next 2 hdc; rep from ***** to last hdc; sc in last hdc. Turn. *(56 cls)*

Row 8: Ch 3, sc in first sc; *****sk next cl and next hdc, cl in next sc; rep from ***** to last sc; sc in last sc. Turn.

Rows 9–11: Rep Row 8.

Row 12: Ch 3, hdc in first sc and in each rem st. Turn. *(170 hdc)*

Row 13: Ch 3, dc in first hdc; *X-st over next 3 hdc; rep from * to last hdc; dc in last hdc. Turn.

Rows 14–17: Rep Row 2.

Row 18: Ch 3, hdc in first dc, in each rem dc and in each ch-1 sp. Turn.

Row 19: Ch 3, hdc in each hdc. Turn.

Row 20: Ch 1, sc in first hdc; * ch 1, sk next hdc, sc in next hdc; rep from * to last hdc; sc in last hdc. Turn.

Row 21: Ch 3, dc in first sc; *2 dc in each of next 4 ch-1 sps; **pc** *(see Pattern Stitches)* in next ch-1 sp; rep from * to last 4 ch-1 sps; 2 dc in each of next 4 ch-1 sps; dc in last sc. Turn. *(16 pcs)*

Row 22: Ch 1, sc in first dc; * ch 1, sk next st, sc in next st; rep from * to last dc; sc in last dc. Turn.

Row 23: Ch 3, hdc in first sc, 2 hdc in each ch-1 sp; hdc in last sc. Turn. *(170 hdc)*

Row 24: Ch 3, hdc in first hdc and in each rem hdc. Turn.

Rows 25–96: Rep Rows 1–24 three more times.

Rows 97–114: Rep Rows 1–18.

Border

Row 1 (RS): Ch 1; in first hdc work (sc, ch 2, sc)—corner made; † ch 1, sk next hdc, sc in next hdc †; rep from † to † to last hdc; in last hdc work (sc, ch 2, sc)—corner made; working across next side, ch 1, sk Row 114, sc in next row; †† ch 1, sk next row, sc in next row ††; rep from †† to †† to last row; working across next side in unused lps of beg ch, in first lp work (sc, ch 2, sc)—corner made; ††† ch 1, sk next lp, sc in next lp †††; rep from ††† to ††† to last lp; in last lp work (sc, ch 2, sc)—corner made; working across next side, ch 1, sk Row 1, sc in next row; rep from †† to †† to first sc; join in first sc; sl st in next ch-2 sp. Turn.

Row 2: Ch 2 *(counts as an hdc)*, in same sp work (hdc, ch 2, 2 hdc)—corner made; *2 hdc in each ch-1 sp to next corner ch-2 sp; in corner ch-2 sp work (2 hdc, ch 2, 2 hdc)—corner made; rep from * twice more; 2 hdc in each ch-1 sp to beg ch-2; join in 2nd ch of beg ch-2. Turn.

Row 3: Ch 1, sc in first hdc; * ch 2, sk next hdc, X-st over next 3 hdc; ch 2, sk next hdc, sc in next hdc; rep from * around, adjusting reps so X-sts are worked over center hdc and ch-2 sps of corners; join in first sc.

Fasten off and weave in all ends.

Blooming Pineapples

EASY

Design by Ruth Shepherd

Size
About 40 x 60 inches

Materials
Medium (worsted) weight yarn,
    41 oz (2870 yds, 1230g) off-white
Note: *Our photographed model
was made with Red Heart Classic,
Off-White #3.*
Size I/9/5.5mm crochet hook or size
    required for gauge
Size G/6/4mm crochet hook
Tapestry needle

Gauge
With larger hook
motif =11 x 10 inches

Pattern Stitch

Puff Stit ch (puff st)
Keeping last lp of each dc on
hook, 3 dc in st or sp indicated,
yo and draw through all 4 lps
on hook.

Instructions

First Motif

Pineapple Center
With larger hook, ch 8, join to form
a ring.

Row 1: Ch 2 *(counts as an hdc)*, 4
hdc in ring—base of pineapple made. (*5 hdc*) Turn.

Row 2: Ch 3 *(counts as a hdc and ch-1 sp)*, [hdc in next
hdc, ch 1] 3 times; hdc in 2nd ch of turning ch-2. Turn.

Row 3: Ch 3, [hdc in next hdc, ch 1, hdc in next ch-1
sp, ch 1] twice; hdc in next hdc, ch 1, hdc in 2nd ch of
turning ch-3. Turn.

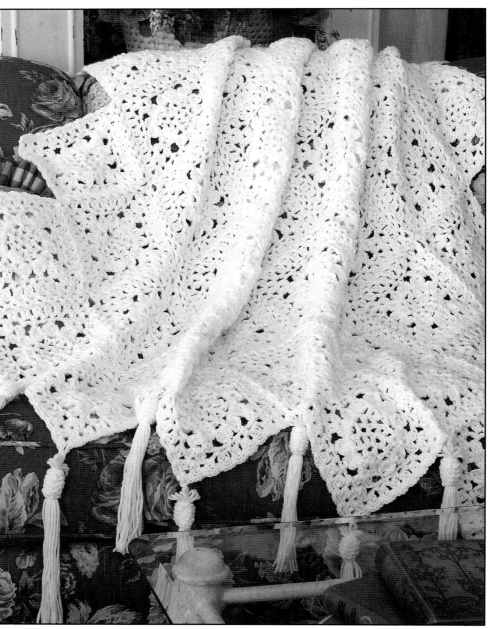

Row 4: Ch 3, sk next ch-1 sp, hdc in next ch-1 sp, ch 1,
hdc in next ch-1 sp, ch 1, hdc in next hdc, [ch 1, hdc
in next ch-1 sp] twice; ch 1, hdc in 2nd ch of turning
ch-3. Turn.

Row 5: Ch 3, sk next ch-1 sp, next hdc and next ch-1 sp,
[hdc in next hdc, ch 1] 3 times; hdc in 2nd ch of turning
ch-3. Turn.

Row 6: Ch 3 *(counts as a dc)*, keeping last lp of each hdc
on hook, hdc in next 3 hdc, yo and draw through all 4
lps on hook; dc in 2nd of turning ch-3. Turn.

Edging

Rnd 1: Ch 3, in first dc work [**puff st** *(see Pattern Stitch)*, ch 3, sl st]; working along side in sps at ends of rows, in each of next 5 rows work (sl st, ch 3, puff st, ch 3, sl st); sk Row 1, in beg ch-8 ring work (2 sc, ch 3, 2 sc); working along next side in sps at ends of row, sk Row 1, in each of next 5 rows work (sl st, ch 3, puff st, ch 3, sl st); join in first ch of beg ch-3.

Rnd 2: Sl st in next 2 chs and in next puff st, ch 3 *(counts as a dc on this and following rnds),* in same puff st work (dc, ch 2, 2 dc)—beg corner made; * ch 3, [sc in next puff st, ch 3] twice; in next puff st work (2 dc, ch 2, 2 dc)—corner made; rep from * twice more; ch 3, [sc in next puff st, ch 3] twice; join in 3rd ch of beg ch-3.

Rnd 3: Sl st in next dc and in next ch-2 sp, beg corner in same sp; * † [ch 3, sc in next ch-3 sp, ch 3, sc in next sc] twice; ch 3, sc in next ch-3 sp, ch 3 †; in next corner ch-2 sp work corner; rep from * twice more, then rep from † to † once; join in 3rd ch of beg ch-3.

Rnd 4: Sl st in next dc and in next ch-2 sp; beg corner in same sp; *2 hdc in each of next 6 ch-3 sps; corner in next corner ch-2 sp; 2 hdc in each of next 6 ch-3 sps; join in 3rd ch of beg ch-3.

Rnd 5: Sl st in next dc and in next ch-2 sp; in same sp work (2 sc, ch 2, 2 sc)—sc corner made; ch 3; * † [sc between next 2 hdc groups, ch 3] 7 times †; in next corner ch-2 sp work (2 sc, ch 3, 2 sc)—sc corner made; rep from * twice more, then rep from † to † once; join in first sc.

Fasten off and weave in ends.

Diagram

Second Motif

Work same as First Motif through Rnd 4 of Edging.

Rnd 5: Sl st in next dc and in next ch-2 sp; in same sp work (2 sc, ch 2, 2 sc)—sc corner made; ch 3; [sc between next 2 hdc groups, ch 3] 7 times; 2 sc in next corner ch-2 sp; ch 1; hold WS of completed motif facing WS of working motif, carefully matching bases of pineapples; on completed motif, sl st in corresponding corner ch-2 sp, ch 1; on working motif, 2 sc in same corner sp; † ch 1; on completed motif, sl st in next ch-3 sp, ch 1; on working motif, sc between next 2 hdc groups †; rep from † to † 6 times more; ch 1; on completed motif, sl st in next ch-3 sp, ch 1; on working motif, 2 sc in next corner ch-2 sp; ch 1; on completed motif, sl st in next corner ch-2 sp, ch 1; on working motif, 2 sc in same corner ch-2 sp; ch 3, [sc between next 2 hdc groups, ch 3] 7 times; corner in next corner ch-2 sp; ch 3, [sc between next 2 hdc groups, ch 3] 7 times; join in first sc.

Fasten off and weave in ends.

Third-Fiftieth Motifs

Referring to Assembly Diagram for placement, work rem motifs as Second Motif, joining adjacent sides in same manner and making sure all four-corner joinings are secure.

Pineapple (make 22)

With smaller hook, ch 5; join to form a ring.

Rnd 1: Ch 1, 8 sc in ring; join in first sc.

Rnd 2: Ch 1, sc in each sc. Do not join.

Rnds 3 & 4: Rep Rnd 2.

Rnd 5: Ch 1, sc in each sc; join in first sc.

Fasten off, leaving a 10-in ch end for sewing.

Pineapple Tassels (make 20)

Cut ten 20-in ch lengths of yarn for each pineapple. Fold lengths in half; pull folded end ¾-in ch up through top of pineapple. Thread tapestry with yarn end and weave through sts of last rnd. Pull up tightly. Insert needle up through center of pineapple, wrap yarn around top of center 2 lps and secure, spreading rem lps on each side. Rep with rem pineapples. Sew one tassel to each point and one to each motif joining on each short end of afghan.

Crystal Lace

EASY

Design by Diane Poellot

Size
About 74 x 51 inches

Materials
Medium (worsted) weight yarn,
41 oz (2870 yds, 1230g) off-white
Note: *Our photographed afghan was made with Red Heart TLC Essentials, White #2316.*
Size I/9/5.5mm crochet hook or size required for gauge
Tapestry needle

Gauge
motif = 5 inches square

Instructions

First Motif

Rnd 1: * Ch 10, sl st in 10th ch from hook—ch-10 lp made; ch 1, 7 sc in ch-10 lp just made; rep from * 3 times more; join to base of first ch-10 lp as follows: remove hook; making sure lps are not twisted, place ends tog keeping 7-sc sides of lps to inside; insert hook in last ch of first lp and draw dropped lp through.

Rnd 2: Ch 1, working over joining in sp between last ch-10 lp made and first ch-10 lp, work (sc, ch 5, sc); 7 sc in next ch-10 lp; *working between ch-10 lps, work (sc, ch 5, sc); 7 sc in next ch-10 lp; rep from * twice more; join in first sc.

Rnd 3: Sl st in next 2 chs of next ch-5 sp, ch 1, in same sp work (sc, ch 5, sc); * † ch 5, sk next 3 sc, sc in next sc, ch 5, sk next 3 sc †; in next ch-5 sp work (sc, ch 5, sc); rep from * twice more, then rep from † to † once; join in first sc.

Rnd 4: Sl st in next ch-5 sp, ch 1, in same sp work (2 sc, ch 3, 3 sc, ch 3, 2 sc)—corner made; * † in each of next 2 ch-5 sp work (3 sc, ch 3, 3 sc) †; in next ch-5 sp work (2 sc, ch 3, 3 sc, ch 3, 2 sc)—corner made; rep from * twice more, then rep from † to † once; join in first sc. Fasten off.

Second Motif

Rnds 1–3: Rep Rnds 1–3 of First Motif.

Rnd 4: Sl st in next ch-5 sp, ch 1, in same sp work (2 sc, ch 3, 3 sc, ch 3, 2 sc)—corner made; *in each of next 2 ch-5 sp work (3 sc, ch 3, 3 sc); in next ch-5 sp work (2 sc, ch 3, 3 sc, ch 3, 2 sc)—corner made; rep from * once more; in each of next 2 ch-5 sps work (3 sc, ch 3, 3 sc); in next ch-5 sp work (2 sc, ch 3, 3 sc); ch 1; hold WS of first motif facing WS of working motif and carefully mat ch sts; sl st in corresponding ch-3 sp on first motif; ch 1; on working motif, then rep from † to † once; join in first sc. Fasten off.

Remaining Motifs

Referring to diagram for placement of motifs, work motifs in same manner as Second Motif, joining sides in similar manner and working corner joinings as necessary.

Diagram

How to Check Gauge

A correct stitch gauge is very important. Please take the time to work a stitch gauge swatch about 4 x 4 inches. Measure the swatch. If the number of stitches and rows are fewer than indicated under "Gauge" in the pattern, your hook is too large. Try another swatch with a smaller size hook. If the number of stitches and rows are more than indicated under "Gauge" in the pattern, your hook is too small. Try another swatch with a larger size hook.

Abbreviations & Symbols

beg	begin/beginning
bpdc	back post double crochet
bpsc	back post single crochet
bptr	back post treble crochet
CC	contrasting color
ch	chain stitch
ch-	refers to chain or space previously made (i.e. ch-1 space)
ch sp	chain space
cl	cluster
cm	centimeter(s)
dc	double crochet
dc dec	double crochet 2 or more stitches together, as indicated
dec	decrease/decreases/decreasing
dtr	double treble crochet
fpdc	front post double crochet
fpsc	front post single crochet
fptr	front post treble crochet
g	grams
hdc	half double crochet
hdc dec	half double crochet 2 or more stitches together, as indicated
lp(s)	loops(s)
MC	main color
mm	millimeter(s)
oz	ounce(s)
pc	popcorn
rem	remain/remaining
rep	repeat(s)
rnd(s)	round(s)
RS	right side
sc	single crochet
sc dec	single crochet 2 or more stitches together, as indicated
sk	skip
sl st	slip stitch
sp(s)	space(s)
st(s)	stitch(es)
tog	together
tr	treble crochet
trtr	triple treble
WS	wrong side
yd(s)	yard(s)
yo	yarn over

* An asterisk (or double asterisk **) is used to mark the beginning of a portion of instructions to be worked more than once; thus, "rep from * twice more" means after working the instructions once, repeat the instructions following the asterisk twice more (3 times in all).

† The dagger (or double daggers ††) identifies a portion of instructions that will be repeated again later in the same row or round.

— The long dash is used to indicate a completed stit ch su ch as a decrease, a shell or a cluster.

() Parentheses are used to enclose the number of stitches you should have when the row or round has been completed.

[] Brackets are used to enclose instructions that should be worked the exact number of times specified immediately following the parentheses, su ch as "[2 sc in next dc, sc in next dc] twice." They are also used to set off and clarify a group of stitches that are to be worked all into the same space or stitch, su ch as "in next corner sp work [2 dc, ch 1, 2 dc]."

[] Brackets and () parentheses are used to provide additional information to clarify instructions.

Join—join with a sl st unless otherwise specified.

The patterns in this book are written using United States terminology. Terms that have different English equivalents are noted below.

United States	English
single crochet (sc)	double crochet (dc)
double crochet (dc)	treble (tr)
treble crochet (tr)	double treble (dtr)
triple treble crochet (trtr)	quadruple treble (q[uad] tr)
skip (sk)	miss
slip stit ch (sl st)	slip stit ch (ss) or single crochet
gauge	tension
yarn over (yo)	yarn over hook (YOH)

Skill Levels

BEGINNER
Beginner projects for first-time crocheters using basic stitches. Minimal shaping.

EASY
Easy projects using basic stitches, repetitive stitch patterns, simple color changes and simple shaping and finishing.

INTERMEDIATE
Intermediate projects with a variety of stitches, mid-level shaping and finishing.

EXPERIENCED
Experienced projects using advanced techniques and stitches, detailed shaping and refined finishing.

Metric Chart

INCHES INTO MILLIMETERS & CENTIMETERS (Rounded off slightly)

inches	mm	cm	inches	cm	inches	cm	inches	cm
1/8	3		5	12.5	21	53.5	38	96.5
1/4	6		5 1/2	14	22	56	39	99
3/8	10	1	6	15	23	58.5	40	101.5
1/2	13	1.3	7	18	24	61	41	104
5/8	15	1.5	8	20.5	25	63.5	42	106.5
3/4	20	2	9	23	26	66	43	109
7/8	22	2.2	10	25.5	27	68.5	44	112
1	25	2.5	11	28	28	71	45	114.5
1 1/4	32	3.2	12	30.5	29	73.5	46	117
1 1/2	38	3.8	13	33	30	76	47	119.5
1 3/4	45	4.5	14	35.5	31	79	48	122
2	50	5	15	38	32	81.5	49	124.5
2 1/2	65	6.5	16	40.5	33	84	50	127
3	75	7.5	17	43	34	86.5		
3 1/2	90	9	18	46	35	89		
4	100	10	19	48.5	36	91.5		
4 1/2	115	11.5	20	51	37	94		

CROCHET HOOKS METRIC CONVERSION CHART

U.S.	1/B	2/C	3/D	4/E	5/F	6/G	8/H	9/I	10/J	10½/K	N
Continental-mm	2.25	2.75	3.25	3.5	3.75	4.25	5	5.5	6	6.5	9.0

Standard Yarn Weight System

Categories of yarn, gauge ranges, and recommended needle and hook sizes

Yarn Weight Symbol & Category Names	1 SUPER FINE	2 FINE	3 LIGHT	4 MEDIUM	5 BULKY	6 SUPER BULKY
Type of Yarns in Category	Sock, Fingering, Baby	Sport, Baby	DK, Light Worsted	Worsted, Afghan, Aran	Chunky, Craft, Rug	Bulky, Roving
Crochet Gauge Ranges in Single Crochet to 4 inch	21–32 sts	16–20 sts	12–17 sts	11–14 sts	8–11 sts	5–9 sts
Recommended Hook in Metric Size Range	2.25–3.5 mm	3.5–4.5 mm	4.5–5.5 mm	5.5–6.5 mm	6.5–9 mm	9 mm and larger
Recommended Hook U.S. Size Range	B1–E4	E4–7	7–I-9	I-9–K-10½	K-10½–M-13	M-13 and larger

The above reflect the most commonly used gauges and hook sizes for specific yarn categories.

Stitch Guide

Chain - ch:
YO, draw through lp on hook.

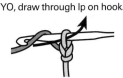

Single Crochet - sc:
Insert hook in st, YO and draw through, YO and draw through both lps on hook.

Reverse Single Crochet -
Reverse sc:
Work from left to right, insert hook in sp or st indicated (**a**), draw lp through sp or st - 2 lps on hook (**b**); YO and draw through lps on hook.

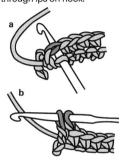

Half Double Crochet - hdc:
YO, insert hook in st, YO, draw through, YO and draw through all 3 lps on hook.

Double Crochet - dc:
YO, insert hook in st, YO, draw through, (YO and draw through 2 lps on hook) twice.

Triple Crochet - trc:
YO twice, insert hook in st, YO, draw through, (YO and draw through 2 lps on hook) 3 times.

Slip Stitch - sl st:
(**a**) **Used for Joinings**
Insert hook in indicated st, YO and draw through st and lp on hook.

(**b**) **Used for Moving Yarn Over**
Insert hook in st, YO draw through st and lp on hook.

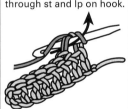

Front Loop - FL:
The front loop is the loop toward you at the top of the stitch.

Back Loop - BL:
The back loop is the loop away from you at the top of the stitch.

Post:
The post is the vertical part of the stitch.

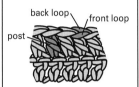

Overcast Stitch is worked loosely to join crochet pieces.

American School of Needlework ®
excellence in instruction

DRG Publishing
306 East Parr Road
Berne, IN 46711
©2004 American School of Needlework
TOLL-FREE ORDER LINE or to request a free catalog (800) 582-6643
Customer Service (800) 282-6643, Fax (800) 882-6643

Visit AnniesAttic.com.

Customer Service (800**) 282-6643, fax (**800**) 882-6643**

We have made every effort to ensure the accuracy and completeness of these instructions. We cannot, however, be responsible for human error, typographical mistakes or variations in individual work.

ISBN:1-59012-097-3   All rights reserved.   Printed in USA   3 4 5 6 7 8 9